JAMES ANGUS

D. H. MacIsaac

Copyright © 2022 by D.H. MacIsaac

All rights reserved. No part of this book may be reproduced in any form or by any electronic or mechanical means, including information storage and retrieval systems, without permission in writing from the publisher, except by a reviewer who may quote brief passages in a review.

Edited by Alisa Brooks

Cover design by SYR Creative

ISBN 979-8-9854624-0-1 (paperback)

First Edition: March 2022

Published by Leah MacIsaac-Ruff

Dedicated to my daughter, to clarify the myths and legends of her great-grandfather.

To M.L., Sam, R.J., and Ron, remembering Quebec Street.

To my wife, for enduring the many repetitions made over the past 50-plus years.

With love.

D.H.

Table of Contents

Chapter 1..8
Chapter 2..12
Chapter 3 15
Chapter 4..20
Chapter 5... 26
Chapter 6..30
Chapter 7..33
Chapter 8..39
Chapter 9..43
Chapter 10..51
Chapter 11..55
Chapter 12..58
Chapter 13..61
Chapter 14 65
Chapter 15 67
Chapter 16.. 70
Chapter 17.. 72

Chapter 18 75
Chapter 19 77
Chapter 20 80
Chapter 21 83
Chapter 22 87
Chapter 23 91
Chapter 24 94
Chapter 25 99
Chapter 26 102
Chapter 27 104
Chapter 28 107
Chapter 29 109
Epilogue 112

To Cheryl:

Thanks for the memories of family & end of life.

Harvey

Chapter 1

HE STOOD OUT among the passengers on the boat from Antigonish to the Cape. He was six inches taller and over seventy-five pounds heavier than anyone around him, and he stood straight, smiling as he watched the summer sun hit the land where he was born. Memories flooded him of the knock-kneed big kid who had to learn to protect himself. Always a target for bullies because of his size, he made up for his lack of speed by mental quickness and strength. Then he thought of his cousins and neighbors, who would be excited to see him. Very few ever ventured away from family and the close-knit Scottish Catholic clan roots, and when those that did came back, they were revered as adventurers. Returning from the west, the striking figure had a sureness bordering on cockiness. He was looking forward to renewing some old ties.

His mother had died, but his father still lived a simple farm life, maintaining the farm with the help of relatives and neighbors. His brother had gone into the priesthood and his two sisters were married and looking after their families, so he no longer fit into any of their lives. He had debated about coming back, but he had to show that he had mastered his life and was ready to cut the cords for good. This summer would be dances and parties, fiddles and drinking; a time of relishing in fun and pranks before heading back west. *One good fling*, he thought. He remembered the girls from point Port Hawkesbury to Inverness, and he wondered how many had married in the five years since he'd been back. At almost thirty years of age, this would be the last visit home. He wondered how many would remember him.

The island men were tall and lean and hungry, but outgoing. They loved to talk and visit. Those from Judique were known as men who loved to dance, and of whom it was said "Judiques on the floor, who will take them off?" Many mainland dances had ended with a challenge to the locals to stand up for their ladies. His friends may have scores to settle, so he would have to watch where he went. He smiled; it looked like a good summer ahead. He took a deep breath, smelt the clean air, and listened to the music in the wind that made home so familiar and inviting.

As the boat neared the dock, he heard the commotion, the shouted questions of visitors asking about their luggage and their destinations. They were from the hot and humid eastern American cities, mainly from the Boston area. Well-heeled and trailing maids and servants, they acted like they had more than they did. These were not the elite of Cape Cod, but were still well enough off to escape the city and its heat and stench of summer.

Cool breezes down the bay, good fishing, fine fresh food, and lazy days made Cape Breton an enjoyable summer prospect. It had an imitation Cape Cod atmosphere. Boating and tea times filled the days and large dinners ended the nights, slowing time to an enjoyable pace. The locals were quaint in their language and customs. Speaking Gaelic was the only inconvenience for those visiting, and some banned the use of the language in their presence, afraid they were being talked about. The Boston people had to control their lives.

Louise was one of those coming with her father and mother from Boston. She was barely five feet tall, but spoiled and outspoken. She was a spirit to be handled. Always catered to by her father, and trained by her mother for the better life, she demanded the attention of everyone she came into contact with. She had a temper that she hid behind petite enchantment. A beauty in a small package, she knew how to take advantage of her position and allure. The last two summers had been spent in the city due to Mother not feeling well enough to travel, and her friends had become boring. So the Cape should be interesting to say the least. She would not allow it to be boring. If it was, she would spice it up—mother be damned. First, she was going to take it easy and find out where to be seen and who to be seen with. That may take some time. Nobody suspected that this sweet, demure father's girl was a spring about to explode.

The boat stopped and JA looked to see who was on the dock. God, they all looked the same! Except for a few spare pounds here and there, they were the same lean, hungry guys he'd grown up with. Completely disinterested in anything happening, they didn't lift their heads and spoke to each other in muffled tones. They shuffled as if there were weights on their feet. *They can't wait to have a drink*, he thought. Stupid Capers never smiled unless they had a drink, and then they wouldn't quit talking until the morning sun. He watched them unload the visitors' trunks and direct the visitors, wondering if they saw him. He stepped forward, reached down, and touched a shoulder. Sandy MacDonald's head snapped back. "Big Jim!" he bellowed. They all came alive with noise and chatter as they saw the big man step onto the wharf. They dropped what they were doing and left the customers standing and staring as they scrambled to greet the returning fellow Caper. Commotion and chaos reigned for a few hectic minutes until Louise yelled, "Where is my trunk?" Then they remembered what they had to do and went back to work, all the time smiling and thinking, "It will be a good time. Big Jim is back."

Chapter 2

OH, WHAT A MORNING! Blue skies, white clouds, clean air, and the sound of axes in the woods. Big Jim felt every blow of the axe brightly in his aching head. But it was too beautiful a day to miss on account of the shindig last night. Everybody had been talking at once, trying to bring him up to date on their lives and telling him who was here, there, or everywhere. Then they were asking him about the west and the railroad, and about the work in the woods and the mines. All this with beer and whiskey flowing, and fiddles burning out tunes one after the other. He'd forgotten how one person would play, another join in, and then all who were not drinking or talking would start playing and singing. That was when foot-stomping and spoons and fiddles created a warmth that stirred your blood and increased your pulse to an exhilarating pace. It dawned on him afterward that all the relatives and friends who were there last night were men. The only women came just to offer food and then disappeared into the noise and confusion of the night. They seemed to be resigned to the fact that boys will be boys. He washed his face in the rain barrel, put on an old shirt and some pants he'd found left over in the house, and walked out to where the axes were, ready to help his father.

His father had sat and drank and visited last night too. But he was up at the crack of dawn because he always was. He was tired, but always smiled and carried himself erect and proud. "Third generation on the Cape," he would tell everybody in his Gaelic Scottish accent. JA had taken this from him and was also proud of his Scottish heritage.

He made his way to where his father was chopping logs and they nodded to each other. Father pointed to some other axes leaning against the logs. Neither man had much to say, as they knew it to be their last summer together. When they did speak it was Gaelic, as it was the easy, expressive language that they could speak while they felled. Both went to work, and JA selected a double-headed axe. He stood the logs on end and split them with one heavy swing. Oh, he forgot how good that felt! It resounded in his head, but he felt the satisfaction as the wood split to the ground. His muscles relaxed and he took another swing. Now he was in motion and kept an even pace. His strength and size allowed him to do in one swing what many had to take two or three extra ones to get done. One day here with his father would do six days of work for him. He was glad to stretch and swing after the three-week trip from the west.

They finished a row of logs and sat to rest. "How are you keeping since mom died?" JA asked. His father put down the axe, wiped his brow, and crossed himself.

"It isn't easy. The family helps, and I go to all the functions, but it isn't as lively as it was when she was alive." He told his son that there were many invites, and the relatives made the days go by with less pain each day; JA's brother had been here for a while, and JA's sisters were always sending people to check on him. They saw him every week at church, and after he would go to their homes and spend the day with the family. His chickens and cows made him come home every night to do chores, and he enjoyed the quiet solitude of the farm at night. He was busy, but the neighbours were always there to help him if he needed, as they had been before.

"I am alright, son. And I am glad you came. But don't wait on me; enjoy the Cape and your friends. They will want to see you and will have many gatherings. So have fun, and remember who you are and where you come from."

Chapter 3

SHE AWOKE to the bright day shining on her bedroom wall. All she could do was hope that someone had made some breakfast tea. She heard her mother and the maid talking in the kitchen, arranging the chores for the day. "I don't think I want to get involved in that business," she said to herself. But as her eyes got accustomed to the room, she saw her trunks open and full, and she knew she had to think about organizing her wardrobe.

They had told her this place was quaint, but her impression was that it was old and small. There was no glitter, no style! It was secluded and quiet—except for the locals singing on the way home last night after the party. What a weird bunch of people. Definitely not city, and certainly not Boston. The maid, Sarah, knocked and entered.

"Water for your washing, Miss. I will bring your tea right away."

"Good. And when you come back, you can help me with my clothes." She swung her legs over the side of the bed, then remembered that she needed the stool to get down. She had never been in such a big bed before. It must be made for giants.

Sarah came with her tea, and they decided on her clothes for today, and what to wear to be seen that evening. A relative of mother's was having a welcome dinner. It should be a splashy event, and she was sure to find out what prospects were ahead for the summer. Things had to be better than the mess at the wharf yesterday. All the commotion, and that huge tree of a man getting all the attention. Nobody even noticed her until she screamed for her trunks. Everybody had told her that the locals were basic. Now she thought, *How true.*

But no matter how basic the locals and their parties were, she was determined to be the talk of the gathering. Sarah said her father had gone fishing and wouldn't be back until this afternoon. Mother would be cleaning the house to make it perfect in case someone happened by. So she had a lazy day ahead. She would freshen up so she could be at her adorable best.

Annie MacDermid thought, *What a great night it is going to be.*

The Boston families were all so well-dressed and perfect-looking. She couldn't wait to hear stories of what fashions were coming. She was happy on the Cape, but still the excitement of visitors always made her wonder what it was like on the mainland. Imagine eating out, buying clothes made by others, and shopping in real stores. Mind you, MacDonald's store was up-to-date, as they heard. But the news was always late arriving in Cape Breton, so they were never sure of what was the latest. She was looking forward to meeting the ladies who had not been here before, and she always enjoyed watching the boys trying to catch one with their easy-going ways and their good looks. They were generous with their time and very pleasant when they were sober, but then again, some needed false strength to talk to women. And, like all boys, they were always showing who's stronger or faster, and who could sing or dance or play an instrument better. But the stories they told always enchanted the ladies, even those who'd heard them before. So, it would be an interesting night.

Angus, her husband, had said he might travel to JA's father's farm to see if JA was going to be around this way tonight and get some news from the west. Mining and logging were drawing men away out there and it looked prosperous. Too bad JA hadn't been home when his mother died, but at least he came home for his father. It would be good to see him. She left her thoughts for the time being; it would be a good night ahead and she needed to get working or she would not have time to enjoy it with her guests.

JA and his father were resting on the bench in front of the house. His father had a way of drying lamb with some local garlic and onions that made a satisfying snack. As they relaxed, a wagon approached on the farm road. It was Red Angus MacDermid. He eased his wagon to a stop and jumped out.

"*Ciamar a tha thu?*" he asked in Gaelic.

"*Tha gu math ciama a tha thu,*" came the reply.

He strode up to big Jim and hugged him. They both tried to squeeze each other until one said uncle. "It is good to see you," JA said. "You are as strong as I remember."

"Well, I haven't been lollygagging around on my butt in the hotels and bars in the west. It has been hard work farming and fishing, and the winters aren't any easier than before. You remember how that wind is harsh and cold. But it is hot today. Do you have something to wet my whistle?"

"Of course! Father always likes to share his unfermented fruit juice."

"Yeah, that has a way of relaxing your system, winter or summer."

Father said, "I will get some and you can tell us what brought you all the way out here, away from your work."

"Well, I had to see the big guy and get a look at that hairbrush under his nose. Every time I see him somewhere he is swamped with people, so I had to come alone to see him up close. But also, Annie is entertaining the Boston Provinces tonight. About five or six families will be there. We would like you to come and liven up the proceedings. Your stories from the west will keep the Yankees from talking about themselves."

They sat down again with their drinks, and they turned the conversation to family and friends. Red Angus recalled what a great cook JA's mother was, and how her hospitality and generosity made her a friend to everyone. From her kitchen flowed pies and tarts and cakes and cookies in a never-ending chain, filled with the warmth and love that made them so tasty. She baked buns and bread that made men's hearts melt. They remembered her hearty laugh when she was happy and her tearful hugs when she was sad. How much she enjoyed people and life, and how she loved to sing when she was working or walking or in church. The children were special to her, and the community loved her smiles and her songs.

Angus looked at JA and, for the first time he could remember, he saw Big Jim with tears on his cheeks.

"Enough," said his father. "I will give him Champ and the wagon. If he gets drunk, Champ knows the way home."

"We will see you later then," Red Angus said as he jumped on his buggy. "I better get home and tell the women to spruce up. Big Jim is coming!"

Chapter 4

THE CAPERS were getting dressed in their Sunday finest. The men were saying, "It is Tuesday night, what are we fussing for?" The women looked glaringly at them and firmly reminded them that there were visitors from Boston coming and that they needed to make a good impression. "Queen Vic must be amongst them," came the reply.

Annie had never fussed so much. With a family to tend to, she never had the occasion to have an elegant air about her. Her niece was coming to look after the kids, and it was going to be a treat to have a free night without having to fuss about them. She was looking forward to adult conversation. She wasn't the only one; there was a definite buzz around Judique.

The MacDermid house was not a large home compared to others in the neighbourhood, but the three-story house had a good area for entertaining. The entrance was a large open area with a staircase leading upstairs. The parlour had a fireplace with windows overlooking the covered porch and a view of the trees and the bay beyond. The rear of the main floor had a bedroom as well as a kitchen and pantry area. Annie had taken the bed out of that room, so there would be plenty of space to sit, eat, and visit, and room for music to be played and enjoyed. The kitchen counters were covered with food and the pantry bar was well-stocked with all kinds of liquids. Annie reminded Red Angus, "Don't get carried away. The Boston women may just drink tea, so wait to see how much to offer." *How can you have a ceilidh and just drink tea?* he thought, smiling.

The guests arrived; Red Angus and Annie greeted them and set them up in the parlour. They all commented on the nice homey atmosphere and said it was good to be invited out to share a home-cooked meal. Annie, being polite as usual, said it was very special to meet new people and make new friends. A few maids arrived and went right to the kitchen to tend to whatever was needed.

All the families had arrived but one; the father had been fishing and was late arriving home. As the latecomers came up the walk, everyone could see how happy he was. He greeted everyone with a smile while his wife and daughter followed behind him. Annie noticed that the daughter was wearing a bizarre outfit...it looked like pants under a skirt. She was such a little girl but walked with such confidence. *I will have to get to know her,* thought Annie, *at least to find out what she is wearing.*

As they approached the house, Louise whispered to her mother, "Relax. We are not late." Father had been fishing and caught a large tuna, and landing it had taken longer than planned. But mother was fastidious and wanted to make the right impression. *Don't worry,* Louise thought, *we will make an impression. Father will regale them with his fish story, and I will charm them all.*

The dinner talk was spirited. Everybody wanted to hear about the fish that was caught. After dinner, the men separated to the porch and the women to the parlour. As the maids gathered the dishes and Annie organized the chores, Margaret MacDougall took her aside and said, "Let the maids look after things. We have to find out what is going on in Boston." They joined the others as tea and homemade candy squares were served. Annie noticed the young girl sitting with her mother and sat down next to them.

"What kind of outfit is that?" she asked.

"A bicycle skirt," Louise replied. "The latest thing. It gives you freedom of movement. And it's great not to have heavy, tight clothes, especially this time of year."

Annie noticed her blue eyes and girlish smile. She was an engaging girl, confident and a free talker. Not at all like the girls around here. Her mother rattled on about her proficiency on the piano, and all the goals she had set for her daughter. The girl smiled and listened quietly, and Annie thought, *I don't think it will be quite that way. That girl has a definite mind.*

Annie noticed Red Angus on the porch, enjoying their cigars and the brandy he was serving. Red Angus felt the warmth of the brandy and listened to the bakery owner from Boston expound on the fact that the fish he'd caught was the biggest of the year. It was early, but it was still the first and was a definite prize. They were all invited to the icehouse tomorrow to see it for themselves. The Yanks all had tales of the one they'd caught or the one that got away. And each took his turn to enlarge his fish by weight or size.

Time had passed and the sunset had been enjoyed when they noticed that the kitchen and bedroom area in the rear of the house had filled with Gaelic and laughter. The two seemed to go together. Some of the Boston men asked what was happening.

"It's a *ceilidh*, a music time we have here. Sandy and Duncan and John play music, and we dance and sing. It is a great time and relaxes everybody," Red Angus explained.

"Let us take a look," said the baker, excited for this finish to the day he had been enjoying.

JA eased Champ to a stop at the top of the road, where he could see the lights and hear the hum of conversation. He also heard Sandy, Duncan, and John warming up their fiddles. He stepped out of the wagon and told Champ to be good, patting his long-time family friend and putting on the oat bag. He wanted to ensure that Champ could relax and be nourished while he waited. JA brushed out the pleats and straightened his kilt to make sure it was showing correctly fore and aft. His size was all the more striking with his bare legs showing under the large cinch belt. Confidently, he made his way toward the light. He heard the wail of a Scottish lament being played, and remembered the song from his youth with a mind and heart of friends and family. He stood in the doorway of the porch, outlined by the lights, to listen for a moment.

"WHAT IS THAT!"

Louise's scream cut through the noise of the music and the party. "Shush," her mother said, as Red Angus laughed and went to the door to greet his friend.

"Come in, Big Jim, and meet our guests from the mainland. Folks, this is Big Jim. He just returned back from the west and has travelled across the country on the new transcontinental railway."

"Well, we came to listen to music and not me," JA replied, raising his arm to indicate the musicians could resume their playing. They broke into a jig, and soon all was smiles and clapping and the women joining in to sing.

Loise sat in the bedroom area, now ringed with chairs, and watched as the Capers laughed and sang. *Good musicians, and very talented*, she thought. All the training she'd had to be a concert pianist, and they looked like they were born with the knack of playing. Some played with their heads down as if they were embarrassed at being heard. Her hands started to clap and her feet tapped the wood floor to the beat. A man got up and started to dance. His hands were straight down at his side, and his face was without expression, but his feet were moving to and fro with the tempo. Annie passed Louise a plate of desserts, which she declined. But she couldn't help asking, "What is it that they are doing?"

"It is the Cape Breton step dance. The expressionless face and the position of the arms allow people to concentrate on the feet movement. Big Jim is good at that."

Oh my goodness, she thought, *what a sight he must be—a house that dances!*

"I didn't mean to scream when he came in, but it was a sight when all of a sudden the doorway was filled up."

"I understand," said Annie. "The man is proud of who he is and his family, and he walks as tall as he is. But if you ever look into those blue eyes, you will see a generous and warm heart. I know from growing up with him and Angus that he is full of the devil. Sunday Mass was the only peaceful time in the area. But he's as good-hearted as he is impish and big. Big Jim spent the last five years out west working at who knows what and seeing the real west. Every person from here that was out west said they would just mention Big Jim and they would get work or a meal or a bed. He must have made some kind of impression on the westerners. A good, loving mother and a hard-working father, two sisters and a brother. Lots of relatives in the area; everyone knows the family. His one sister sings opera music and has a beautiful voice; her name is Mary MacDonald. The other sister, Jessie Beaton, is as caring and loving as one can be. Interesting family, and very proud of the Scottish Heritage from the Isle of Eigg and from Judique of Inverness County through and through. Anyway, my dear, come and visit me sometime and we will have tea. I look forward to talking more later." And Annie left to make sure dessert was being served.

What warm people, Louise thought. *Open and friendly and close to each other*. The music was playing again, and two women were dancing a jig with happy laughter. The Boston wives were smiling as they looked on. Louis saw her father and mother clapping their hands and enjoying themselves.

"A *ceilidh* is a good time," a deep voice said. She bent backward in her chair to see the man who had spoken.

Chapter 5

HER FIRST IMPRESSIONS were his huge moustache, ruddy complexion, chest, and large head. His size overwhelmed her.

He said, "I did not mean to scare you, but I find that I can't shrink any smaller."

His voice with its deep tones made her feel quite relaxed, and she felt herself settle back into the chair.

"Well, if you were smaller, they couldn't call you Big Jim, could they?"

He laughed and answered, "You are right, they would have to come up with another name."

Looking at his head, she said, "Maybe Wavy Jim with all the waves in your hair."

He laughed again. He found her pretty smile and quick manner relaxed him. "I better go and visit and hear about the fish that was caught."

"My father will be telling that story until Christmas time, so be prepared to hear every gory detail all night."

"Thanks for the warning. Can I bring you anything to drink? That's what I do."

"No thanks. I look forward to seeing you again."

She watched him turn away as someone called him. What a nice feeling she had, flushed and pleased. She was pleasantly happy that she was here.

JA saw Duncan standing against the wall. They shook hands, laughing, and both started to speak at the same time: "How are you?" They laughed again.

Duncan said, "You are all right—you are here!"

"What are you working at?" JA asked.

"Oh, I am at the damn fish plant in Port Hood. Those loyalists up there could stand a good night out and some dancing; they are so uptight. Always picking at something. But it is steady work and decent pay, so it is good until the fall. What are you doing out west?"

"Well, there are a lot of choices out there: mining, logging, fishing—all we do, but 100 times more. They found gold at Barkerville and now there is a lot going there. But I found out that where there are men there is also a need for someone to provide a bed or food or drink. That is what I have learned to do, providing what people need. I find that I can make people happy, and besides, there's good money in it. With all the growth and the people moving in, there is much need to be filled. And it is a really beautiful country. But it needs more of Inverness County to make it real."

"We will look at that. Maybe your cousin Angus and I could go together."

"Yes, what the country needs to stir it up is Crazy Angus! He would bring it to life, for sure."

The music started again, and Duncan left to join in. JA met a few more of the men from the Boston Provinces who were starting to glow with Red Angus' velvet liquid, good food, and lively music. Some were talking louder and quicker than before, telling of their trials and tribulations in the big city. JA listened patiently, nodding and smiling politely, while Red Angus exchanged any empty jar with a full one. The girl's father came forward and shook JA's hand. "Glad to meet you. It must be pretty exciting to travel across the country by train."

"Not as exciting as catching your fish, I bet."

"Nothing other than the birth of my daughter has been so thrilling. It just kept running away from left to right. My arms felt like they could fall off when we finally pulled him to the side of the boat. Even then, it took some time to get him controlled and onto the boat. Amazing! My heart is still beating about a thousand times a minute, it seems."

"Well, that is what vacations on the Cape are all about, so I'm glad it worked out for you."

"And to finish off the glorious day with the people and the conversation tonight is a real treat. Everyone is so warm and friendly. Words seem to flow like water."

"Maybe like a babbling brook sometimes. But they love each other and all their friends, neighbours, and especially new people they meet."

"It is so easy to relax. And the music! It is hard to believe they haven't had much training. My wife has been training my daughter on the piano since she was five or six, and she's progressing very well toward doing a full concert. But it costs money, and these fellows just seem to play."

"They play from the heart and use the methods of their parents and relatives. It is a knack that some become very good at, and they enjoy playing at these parties. They keep it interesting for the crowd. How long are you here?"

"My wife and daughter are here all summer, but I may have to go back earlier if my business needs me. I run three bakeries. You have to watch how the staff handles the problems. What is your line of work?"

"I grew up on a farm, so I learned to be a jack of all trades. But I am afraid I'm not one for boats or fishing. I heard about British Columbia when I went to Ontario. It is a very exciting place—clear skies and clean water, rough terrain, but put it all together and it takes your breath away. I found work providing food and lodging for newcomers and I managed a few places. I like the job because I can help people and earn a living doing very satisfying and fulfilling work."

"You would be good at that, as you have a good, pleasant manner. And your size would keep anyone from taking advantage."

"Well, it does have its benefits. Look at your daughter and one of the MacNeil girls dancing; it looks like she is enjoying it."

"Yes, it does. That is good for her. She needs to laugh and enjoy life. City life and the people there are restrictive in some ways. When we can expand ourselves, we learn."

JA nodded, thinking about her smile, her energy, and her vitality.

Chapter 6

ANOTHER BLUE SKY greeted Louise as she opened her curtains. Nobody was up yet but she couldn't sleep any longer. She had such a happy glow throughout her whole body. Her mind was relaxed, but at the same time it kept going over and over the last two days. She gazed over the bay and saw the fishing boats on the water, the serenity of the billowing clouds, a hawk circling in the sky. She had never been at such ease. What a beautiful peace she felt.

She heard Sarah in the kitchen, stoking the fire, and went to the door to stick her head out.

"Please bring some tea when it is ready. I'm awake."

"Surely Miss, as soon as it is ready. And I will bring the basin to wash."

"Fine, thank you."

She climbed back up onto the bed and lay flat with her eyes wide open, staring at nothing and trying to put her thoughts together. She'd never felt this way before and wondered why and where it had come from.

The people last night were so open, friendly, and talented. She never thought so many people could have so much enjoyment with each other. The stories of the Cape were engaging. These were plain people with pure motives, driven to survive each day and provide for their families. And laugh—how they laughed from the soles of their feet! One larger-built lady laughed and Louise had had to laugh too as she watched her whole body shake like jelly with tears running down her cheeks. And Duncan, the fiddle player, always had a smile when he looked her way. His face beamed as he played; he'd enjoyed having an audience that he was able to touch with his music. And the dancers! They were so energetic and gracious, and put so much into their dances.

"Here is your tea and wash water, Miss." Sarah's voice broke the spell.

"Thank you. Tell me, did you enjoy the party last night?"

"Yes, Miss, it was truly a happy place. The work was so easy to do with all the music and singing. You looked like you enjoyed the dancing."

"Yes, it was fun! Life in Boston seems so far away. But this was such a good time, it will be hard to forget. Are mother and father up yet?"

"No. I will take the basin as soon as they are ready. Your father had such a big day, fishing and all, and your mother was tired from worrying and organizing everything. It will be a good day for them to relax and settle in."

"Maybe for you, but I will get dressed and go for a walk in the village just to enjoy the day. Then I can sit by the water and enjoy the quiet. It will be a good day."

"By the way, Miss, that big man there last night was quite a giant. He made the maids scared when he came in, he was so big. And that skirt he was wearing showed those trunks for legs. His hair was so wavy and that big moustache...I have never seen such a sight!"

"Yes, but did you see those eyes? Bluer than the sea, so deep and soft and clear. I couldn't look away from them. I didn't even see what he was wearing; all I remember is his eyes and his size."

"We all laughed when you screamed when you saw him. That was a moment that would have scared us all, if I can say so."

"It is all right to say that here, but I would not repeat it in Boston."

"No, Miss. Surely forgotten when we leave."

"They say he can dance and is quite athletic. I wonder if he will be at the games two Saturdays away."

"Yes, Miss, the men were talking about whether he could beat their Irish boy, Paddy Clark, so it will be something to look forward to seeing. I better go and get the water ready for your mother and father. I will check back if you need any help to dress."

"Thank you. I will drink my tea and just think about last night."

She wondered why she remembered his eyes and felt herself blush. Good heavens, why did she feel that way? *Control yourself. You are only here for the summer. Now get dressed and go for a walk, it will get the silly feeling out of you.* But his eyes were so blue and deep.... Oh, well. She would have a lot to do while she was here, and plenty of other things to think about. *Come on, Louise, get ready and go out,* she told herself.

Chapter 7

HE WAS CHOPPING WOOD with his dad, and they were talking about the party.

"I knew you had a good time," his dad laughed, "when I found you asleep in the wagon with a big smile on your face. I heard you arrive in the wee hours. You must have sung for over half an hour before you fell asleep, though Champ and I were the only ones that heard you. You sing and laugh like your mother. I am glad you are able to enjoy life like she did. You may be big like me in stature, but you have her warmth of heart and love of life. Don't lose it."

He set down his axe. "Listen, we are caught up for the day, and I have to go to MacDonald's to see about a new cow as mine is drying up. Why don't you wander into town and see who is there? It will be good for you."

"Yes, I want to talk to Red Angus about the games, as he said he wants me to throw the hammer. Something about the Boston Provinces people having a group of Irish ones come to challenge us. There's talk about a wager or two. I will go for a walk and see what plans are up."

JA washed in the rain basin and thought about what to wear. Something light but still dressy. And his bowler hat; it made him look taller—as if he needed that. A bow tie and a jacket would be just right.

He dressed and started to walk. In the Cape Breton sunlight, he felt the need to hum and sing to himself. As he got closer to town, he began to recognize old neighbours, and found himself waving and greeting people over and over again.

"Hello, Big Jim!" he heard, and Dugald came up and grasped his hand. "I am glad you have come home. It is good to see you. Jessie and Mary didn't say anything!"

"No, I just felt I had to come back and see everybody. I plan to see Jessie tomorrow, and Mary I will see on Sunday at Mass and dinner after. They know I'm here, but they are busy with their families and kids and everything. How have you been?"

"Alice and I have been doing well, and we often think of you out there in the west and what a change and a challenge that would be."

Yes, quite a change, JA thought. Alice and Dugald would never think beyond Port Hood or Port Hawkesbury. But they are happy, so to each his own.

"Well, I am on my way to see John at the store, so we will see you on Sunday."

As he approached the store, he heard a yell but couldn't see anyone. The door of the store burst open and there came Angus, his cousin. Little Angus, they called him—or Crazy Angus. He was a bundle of energy bursting with life and amazement.

"JA, you big, overgrown weed! How the hell are you?" He raced toward JA, and JA picked him up and swung him around and over his head.

"Whoa, big guy. One more swing and last night's party may arrive."

"How is my happy little cousin? Still teasing the girls and causing the priests to avoid confession? Keeping the Cape from becoming boring?"

"Oh, you know how the people just all like a good drink, all the right stuff, but someone has to stir it up. By the way, Duncan told me about the party last night at Red Angus'. It seemed that you stirred up the proceedings yourself. He said he just about laughed himself silly when that young girl screamed when you came through the door. The boys will be telling that story all winter long, every time the amber fluid is flowing."

"Yes, I guess it was a shock for her. She is such a tiny thing, and she was sitting, and I never think about my size. I know with babies and young kids I have to be careful not to overwhelm them. But she recovered and had a good time, she danced and enjoyed the boys playing."

"Yes, Duncan said she was really following them as they played. I hear she is a little one, but quite forward, dressed in different clothes. If only I was younger."

"Well, I think she would be more than a Caper could handle. Anyhow, I am going in to see John and whoever else is in the store."

"Just John now, but he has the tea on so go and have a visit. I have to get back to work. I will see you Sunday at the latest."

As JA entered the store he greeted John in Gaelic, and they both hugged. "Have some tea and half milk?"

"Some habits never change. How is business?"

"Too bad. And I still have the band, we play most nights at the hotel. It is enjoyable. And of course, we raise the flag each morning and lower it each night."

"Still an event to behold on the Cape, for sure. Any good cigars?"

"Yes, let me give you a couple for a homecoming present. Take these."

Just then the door opened, and the sunlight shone into the store. There stood Louise.

"Come in, Miss," said John. "May I help you?"

"I am a summer visitor, just come to see what's in the village."

"Well, not much other than the post office, our store, a ladies' shop, and a men's haberdasher. But we have good general goods and groceries."

"Well, mother and the maid are more for that. I may go and look at the ladies' shop."

JA then stepped forward and said, "Hello again. I'm walking that way. Would you like some company?"

"I didn't see you there, but I don't know how I could miss you. That would be nice."

"I am going to have tea. Could I interest you in joining me?"

"Yes, that would be refreshing."

"Sit on the bench and I will bring it right out."

When he brought the drinks, he noticed again how bright and smiling she was. She reminded him of a China doll. He passed her the drink and sat at the far end of the bench.

"It is a very quaint place," she said.

"Yes, but the people make it live. They're very hospitable to everyone." He how she sat erect and looked straight at him.

Those eyes are so blue, she thought, *and such a big head and shoulders.* "I hear that there are going to be some games in two Saturdays. Are you one who takes part?"

"Well, I wasn't planning anything, but some have asked me. So I will have to decide. I used to run but I'm not too fast any longer. So if I play, I will throw the hammer."

"What is that?" she asked, trying to be less obvious as she stared at him.

"Well, the hammer is a chain with a 50-pound (or so) ball on the end, and you spin it a few times, then let it go as far as you can. It takes balance and power."
That pretty well fits you, she thought. "Thanks for the drink. I better go to the ladies' shop."

"You are welcome anytime. It would be my pleasure."

He lifted his hat as he rose and, as she walked away, he felt the feeling from last night: relaxed and comfortable. He was used to talking to men; this was a delight.

I should go down to the water, he thought. The tide was in and there was a cool breeze on the bay. He strolled and found a rock to sit on in the shade. The quiet of the waves and the pleasant salt air smell relaxed him. He would rest, and then go home and help his father with the evening chores. They had plans to see Jessie and Mary, and he must make sure he left himself enough time. He closed his eyes and listened to the melody of the waves on the shore.

"BOO!"

He jumped up and there stood Louise, smiling mischievously. "Just getting even for last night."

"I guess that was to be expected."

"I saw you here and it looked so natural. I hope you don't mind me interrupting your thoughts?"

"No, I was just enjoying the waves. Sit down and close your eyes and listen." She sat on the rock next to him and did as he asked. She heard the continuous, soothing pattern of the waves, and it reminded her of the piano concertos she played. When she opened her eyes, he was smiling at her. She decided right then and there that she was going to make sure she spent as much time as she could in his company.

"I suppose you have a lot of people to visit and a busy schedule."

"Just to make sure I spend time with my father, and my two sisters and their husbands. Every Sunday is Mass, and then the games are in two weeks. But there is always a *ceilidh* or two. It is pretty much what comes."

"How far do you live from the bay?"

"About one half mile up the road on the right, uphill a little, but a decent spot."

"Maybe my family will come by and visit one day."

"Yes, anytime. The door is always open."

"I better go now. Thanks for letting me share the water with you, but my father and mother will be wondering where I am."

"Well, take care. It was nice seeing you."

As he watched her walk away, he reached into his pocket, pulled out one of the cigars, and lit it. He thought, *this is going to be a good summer.*

Chapter 8

JA MET WITH RED ANGUS at the stairs of the church. "The games are on, the Provinces versus the Cape. They are bringing a group of Irish guys and they want to compete on everything—even the hammer throw."

"Who are they bringing? Anyone we should worry about?"

"They are talking about a fireman named Paddy Clark. He is their hope. He will throw the hammer against you, and they want to double up all the bets for that event."

"Thanks for the pressure. I thought I was here on holidays. I guess I will have to practice with father when I'm doing the chores."

"Don't worry, JA, we all know what you can do. We know you will win."

"Well, when you go to church today, just pray a little harder; it can't hurt. I'm going to see Mary and Jessie after church, so we will talk more tomorrow."

After Mass, he waited for Mary, her husband Brian, and their four kids. Jessie showed up too, saying that Alex was not feeling well, but she wanted them all to come to the house as she had prepared everything. They agreed, and their father said it would be good to get a cool drink on such a warm day.

Jessie smiled and said, "Of course, Dad. Our family will have a refreshing drink or two to wash away the dust of the day."

The family talked all afternoon, reliving memories of their mother and the growing pains they'd all had. Stories were told of how they walked to school when their father was working. They laughed at how their brother would sometimes drive Champ to school—too fast. He would spill everybody into the snow or dust, whatever was in the schoolyard. Mary and Jessie laughed and said they could never look good, as their clothes and hair were always blown about when he drove.

"It's good that mother didn't know," Jessie said with a smile.

JA said, "She always knew, but never let on. She was only upset when we weren't presentable at church or special events."

"I think she gave up on JA in the end. She would say, 'What am I going to do with him?' Father and her would wonder what they did to deserve you, JA."

"Well, I guess she taught me how to have fun and make people laugh while you two sang."

"Our brother did both. He could make you laugh and he could sing, but he had quiet moments too. I guess that is why he became a priest."

"I remember when you got married, Mary, and Mom was so happy doing everything for you. When the first baby was born, she sang and let everyone know she was a grandmother. You would never know Brian and his family had anything to do with it. It was her daughter's child and it was hers."

They then talked about JA and his trip west. He said he felt at home there. Jessie said it was attractive to her and Alex them because of his health. JA said that if they came, he would help where he could. Mary said, "You guys going out there too and leaving me at home with four kids?"

They laughed. "Brian will always look after you," said Jessie. "And you know that the Cape has too much hold on you," added JA.

"Yes, I was talking to the Provinces people and with all the goods they have I still feel better off staying here. By the way, JA, every time I see anyone they mention 'that girl.' They call her 'the snob' or 'brat' or 'spoiled kid.' What is happening there?"

Jessie added that she noticed in church that the girl only smiles at JA or at them, but not at anyone else.

"And the clothes she wears are so bright! She walks around Judique like she owns it."

"And always seems to find you, JA. So watch out. She is everywhere you are these days."

"Well, I enjoy her. I can talk to her like one of the boys, so easy. And when she laughs her eyes shine."

"A bad sign, JA. She is too young for you. Watch out."

"Well, you two take care of me too well. So know I will be careful here, and look after the Capers when I go back to the west. I may have to get ready for the games, so I will be kept busy. Red Angus told me today that they are making big wagers on me. The Provinces are to bring a big Irish guy, so I will just throw the hammer and see what happens. It is only next Saturday, so when you go to prayers this week say an extra one for me. Whatever happens there it will be a party afterward where the noise is bound to be heard all the way to Boston. Weeping or rejoicing, it will be a party."

Chapter 9

THE BIG SATURDAY ARRIVED, and like all Caper Saturdays of importance, the sky was blue and a breeze was blowing in from the bay. Capers knew that you could always tell when something special was about to happen; the exceptional weather days were reserved for the gathering of the clans, weddings, and games weekends. The anticipation grew from the first morning sun on the dew. JA and his father sat on the log bench in front of the house and listened to the area come alive.

"Today is the day, my boy. It was a day like this when I married your mother, and when you were born. No matter what happens, make yourself proud of who you are."

"Father, you have trained me to do my best. The boys who are competing against the Provinces are all game and ready to go. Look, it sounds like John's band is getting ready to play, with the flag going up now. That might wake up the Yanks! The pipes will be tuning; it sounds like the Highlands would have. It will be quite a show. Even Champ knows something is going to happen; look at him prancing back and forth—he doesn't want to miss it!"

"When do you compete today?"

"At the last, as the boys want to either collect all the losses back or double up on their winnings."

"A lot of pressure on you, my son—but it will be exciting."

"Yes, they even imported a sprinter from Port Hood, a young man named Smith."

"Probably named David if he is from there."

"They have Donald MacNeil to toss the caber, and the boys from Cheticamp to run the marathon. A strong bunch of competitors. MacNeil and I are anchoring the tug-of-war with Red Angus, Dugald, Big Sandy, and a fellow from Port Hawkesbury whom I haven't met yet."

"Another test, before we get ready?"

"No, I think I will go talk to Champ and get him ready for the trip. You have your tea and then we can clean up and get an early start. Don't forget your kilt and vest so that they know what side you are on."

"I don't think anyone will take us as being from the Provinces."

"Not with a drink in your hand, they won't!"

"Is that girl going to be there?"

"Of course. Her family is excited about showing some culture to the Cape. They will be front and centre. Why do you ask?"

"You've seen quite a bit of her, and she follows like a kitten ready to pounce...or like a lion stalking its prey."

"Well, I enjoy her company. She makes me feel bigger than I am, more free. She and I enjoy the *ceilidh* and the other gatherings, so it will be the same today. Gives me someone to look forward to seeing. Along with Mary and Jessie, with their families and lots of supporters."

"Don't forget Crazy Angus, your cousin, will be entertaining everybody with his antics all day."

"And most of the night. It is a good thing that Mass isn't until 11:00 tomorrow or it would be a sparse bunch for Father Martin."

"He is Irish. He wouldn't notice anyway."

"Time for us to get ready. We can leave when we are all together."

"When we come, father, they will know it is time to start."

Louise picked out brightly coloured clothing so she would be easy to spot in the crowd. As she spread them out on her bed, her mother entered the room, asking, "Can I talk to you for a minute?"

"Yes, of course. I am just getting ready for today."

"Well, I am concerned about today. Your father and I are wondering which side you will be cheering for today. The people from Boston are expecting us to support them and the way you have been following that giant around...well, they're asking what is going on."

"I am happy when he is around, and I look forward to watching him today."

"Remember, Louise: we are going back home, and this will be a summer memory. We have your lessons, and you will soon be getting opportunities to let everyone see your talent. We've spent a lot of time and money to get you to this point. We want you to succeed. You must look after yourself."

"Mother, I am okay. He makes me feel good and I am happy being around him. Don't worry! I want to enjoy today. Boston will come soon enough."

"Just remember what I said. We just want you to be happy and have a good life."

"Okay, mother. Now let's get ready or we will be late for the ceremonies."

The crowd was busy greeting one another. The ones from the Provinces went to the shady part of the park. The other side was more open, with a slope going down to a creek. The Capers smiled as they stored the drinks—water and otherwise—in the cool running water. The pipes continued tuning, and a drumroll like the calling of animals to their pride was heard. The excitement was high as the Provinces' finery spread out under the trees contrasted with the white aprons of maids preparing the food and serving their patrons. The Caper wives and their children scurried around, setting up the food and laying out blankets on the ground. The contrast between the groups was accentuated by the flags over each section. The men from the Provinces arrived with their contestants. They wore stylish uniforms with matching leggings.

The Caper men were sitting and watching things evolve when crazy Angus said, "It is a proud man over there who will be very sorry when we finish the day. The boys from Cheticamp have been ready to run for two days. They're like spirited horses. And I would put money on Smith, but he's a Protestant and Father Martin would make my confession twice as hard if I bet on him. Alec Beaton and Donald Gillis are going from our side to see what wagers are going to be. The bets are put into the hat and then they match our pot or arrive at the odds. They will send the baker and the tall skinny guy. Our two will be the sober ones, and we know they won't waste any money."

Everything seemed ready and it was relatively quiet when Champ pulled up with JA and his father. "Here is Big Jim!" someone said. "Now we can get started!"

"About time!" a voice from the Provinces replied.

The United Church Minister yelled that the marathon would be the first event. The Cheticamp boys lined up and the Provinces' team came to the gun. "The first man runs up the hill and turns left for half a mile and comes through the pasture to here. The second man leaves when he receives the baton. Two governors, one from each team, will be at each corner to ensure honesty."

The gun sounded and the runners sprinted up the hill. After they were out of sight, the governors called back who was leading and by how much. The Capers headed to the creek to refresh themselves as they waited to hear the results. As the race progressed, they became grimmer, as the Provinces' team continued to lead. The last runners left—they had lost the marathon. Everyone now knew that the Provinces' team was going to be a tough match for the day.

"Now we will have the sprinters up to the line." All eyes looked up the grass pat and there was a gasp from the Capers: their runner, Smith, had three rivals.

"That's not fair!"

"No one said a number," came the reply.

The Provinces' crowd surged forward to watch. The Capers' Smith was between the other two. When the gun sounded, they were all together. In the last ten yards, Smith and the runner on his left bumped and were both thrown off stride. The runner on the right side pulled ahead by a step and broke the tape.

"Tough luck!" yelled the Provinces.

The Caper faces were glum when Annie MacDermid shouted that they needed some fiddle music. Duncan started playing, and the crowd started to sing and dance. Crazy Angus was in the middle with a jar in each hand, not spilling a drop as his feet kicked up the dust. In response the Provinces' camp started singing. Soon the music had both sides laughing, their voices getting louder. The Capers knew they had to win the last two events to collect the bets.

The next one was the tug-of-war. They lined up with MacLean and JA anchoring the Capers. The Boston team came out looking big with Paddy Clark anchoring their team. Clark had shoulders like no one had ever seen, muscles on muscles. JA and MacLean looked down the line as Red Angus said, "It is a formidable task, but our Island pride is on the line." JA's sisters called out and he looked up without smiling. As he did, he noticed Louise smiling at him. He stood a little taller and put his mind to the task of holding the rope and getting his foothold.

Father Martin and the Protestant Minister came to the middle and said that the pull would be six feet to one side or the other. Whoever pulled the flag over six feet would win.

The hankie was raised and dropped, and the rope was so taut it threatened to break. Red Angus' foot slid, and the Provinces gained three feet. JA gave a Gaelic cry and the Capers pulled it even. The crowds on both sides roared with cheers of "PULL, PULL, PULL!"

For the next seven minutes, the rope went one way and then back. JA reached and took another six inches of hold, his muscles bulging as he reached his limit with a mighty tug. MacLean joined in and Red Angus felt the surge reach into his muscles as the Capers overwhelmed their foes. The pull of six feet was won with another Gaelic roar. The Provinces were on their stomachs, gasping, while their supporters wondered what had just happened.

"Fifteen minutes until the caber toss. Refresh yourselves."

All of those in the tug-of-war lay down while water was poured over their exhausted bodies.

"Sorry men," said Red Angus. "I almost lost it for us. My shoe blew into pieces."

"No worry," said MacLean. "JA's cry and power saw us through."

"Anyone seen Crazy Angus with the jars?" someone asked just as Dugald showed up with a handful of jars. "This is the Keith stuff—it is sure to put life back into your veins."

With one tilt JA drained his jar and put it down on the grass. He opened his eyes after a couple of minutes and there were Mary and Jessie clapping their hands. He said, "Your cheers made me pull even harder."

"The Provinces' ladies were saying that they never had lost for over two years. They are still disbelieving it."

"With MacLean on the caber and me on the hammer, it will give us a chance to go for the money."

"Yes. Crazy Angus has gone and is encouraging the bets on you two, so it will be quite a pot when it is over. By the way, Louise was cheering for you and has upset her parents and their friends. I think the mother was already disgusted at the betting, and when Louise started cheering she wanted to leave; but they won't go, so she has to stay. We will go and look after the others. Best of luck!"

Another jar appeared in his line of vision. Louise was holding it out to him. "To the victor! This should help you with the next event."
Her brightness was contagious. "Are you enjoying the games?"

"I haven't seen such men competing like this before. So much strength and control—it is truly amazing."

"I have to go see the caber toss and then I have to get ready for my toss. Thanks for the jar."

"I will be watching closely."

MacLean was a broad man. Not as tall as JA and more stocky, but he had the confidence of a Caper and it showed when he walked. The Capers had their own surprise for the Provinces when they marched out two caber tossers. There were no complaints after the sprint event. MacLean and Roderick James each had two solid tosses and the Capers won handily. The score was even at two wins each. The pot grew bigger.

Chapter 10

JA FINISHED HIS JAR of malt and wiped his brows. He stood up and raised his hands high over his head and then reached for his toes. He laughed to himself, as he could barely reach his ankles. *I've never been able to touch my toes and I never will.* He remembered when he was about twelve and Red Angus would bend him over and push his back down to help him reach his toes: "You are never going to do it JA, you're made all wrong. You are too long in the legs, or your back is too short. And those big knock knees don't help." JA smiled as he stood up, his thoughts moving to the task ahead. He wondered if he could get the motion he would need. He heard someone singing, reminding him of how his mother had a lilt and a smile in her songs, and he felt the tempo and the timing come back. *Just take your time and swing low, go around three times, and let it* *go at the lowest point so that it continues up and away to the highest peak. The distance will come from the push. Relax and think it through—let your thinking put it in place.*

"Hey, JA!" he heard, as Crazy Angus came running up. "The Provinces are piling in the pot. If you win, the Cape will own them. I've never seen so much money. We are all with you because you're our big chance."

JA now looked to the throw box. The crowd was gathering, everyone talking excitedly. They were gesturing and laughing, and the jars were making their voices louder and louder. Capers and the Bostonians were intermingled as they crowded in to see JA and the Clark fellow. JA spotted his sisters and his father, who waved. His father clasped his hands together to show that they were with him. Red Angus approached and said they were ready to start. He hugged JA without a word and walked silently beside him to the throw box. Paddy Clark came from the Boston crowd and they both smiled and extended their hands to each other. JA noticed Clark's black curly hair and smiled to himself as he thought that this man would be good to share a jar or two with some other time. Both men stood at the box.
"The weight is 56 pounds, and both instruments have been weighed and confirmed by both sides. Each man will have three throws and the best throw will be the victor. The visitors from Boston get the choice of going first or second."

"I will go first," said Clark. He strode forward, picked up his chain, and lifted the ball to wipe it clean. Striding to the box, he measured his three steps to the toe line. Working to his starting position he took a deep breath and, grunting, he turned three times and flung the hammer and chain into the blue sky. It seemed to soar forever, but it did eventually land in the field. The crowd cheered as the marker was put down. JA squinted into the field, thinking that the throw was one of the best he had ever seen. Taking a deep breath, he tightened his kilt, raised the ball, wiped it off, and stepped off his paces.

Looking at the ground, he started his motion and, turning three times, released the hammer. It was a good throw and carried like Clark's but was shorter and off-course.

"Boston, by ten feet." The crowd stirred and the commotion around the pot was strong as the bets increased. Clark made his second effort, and it was five feet shorter than his first—but still farther than JA's throw.

JA walked into the box and stepped into his second toss. The height was more than he wanted. The hammer landed near Clark's second. The Capers groaned and the Provinces were clapping and slapping each other on the back.

Clark came forward for his third toss. Smiling, he looked at JA and said, "My best is yet to come." He cleaned his ball and measured his strides. Leaning down, he pulled his hammer up and, swinging around, his release was near perfect. "Boston, five feet farther on!" The crowd exploded with cheers.

JA stretched once more and went for his chain. He looked down when it was handed to him, and saw Louise smiling. "They told me you could do it and I know you can," she said, handing him the hammer. *It weighs almost as much as you*, he thought as he strode into the box. He stepped to the front of the box, to see the markers, and thought that he had gone too high on both. *Less height and more power,* he said to himself. As he started his steps, he felt the surge of his motion, and as he reached the final spin he pushed with his legs. He felt the release go at the proper time. The hammer soared, and everyone gasped at the speed and height as it seemed to continue, like it was suspended in air. Finally, it fell to the ground. All watched as the judges ran to mark it.

"JA by five feet!"

The Capers jumped and yelled, and the Provinces were silent. JA smiled, dropping his arms to his sides. Red Angus was hugging him, cheering and laughing. He threw a towel over JA's head and rubbed his hair. The Capers were around him, patting his back and slapping his arms. He looked for his father, who had a jar raised in salute. JA waved to Mary and Jessie and saw tears in both their eyes. He felt a push from behind, and a tug on his kilt. Looking down, he saw Louise. In one motion he reached down, lifted her up, and hugged her to him with one arm. She put her head on his shoulder and he carried her above the crowd. As they walked she cried, laughed, and waved to the Boston people. She could see her mother frowning as she waited for her father to pay his dues, but it didn't dim her happiness. She was princess for a day!

Chapter 11

THIS WAS TO BE A BIG WEDDING in Boston, an affair that Louise's mother had been planning since her daughter was born. But how did her pretty little girl ever think of marrying this giant bull moose of a man? It wasn't only that the big horse was big—everything about him was big: his hands, his hair, his mustache. Mary Mother of God, what did she see in him? When they came to see her after the party at the church, she knew just by looking at Louise that her arguments would be lost. Her daughter was shining in the night light, and her eyes showed that her heart was captivated. When she asked him what his plans were, and he said going back to the west as soon as he could, she saw Louise sink down. So she asked what his intentions were toward her daughter. JA took Louise's hand in his and said he wanted to marry Louise and have her with him.

"But you can't marry her unless it is in a proper church—and not here, but in Boston. It will take me months to prepare. I have to get the proper priest, send invitations, and do the reception the right way. I need a year at least."

Louise burst into tears and ran from the room.

"Daddy! Daddy, we can't do this!"

Her father had a jar in his hand and smiled as Louise hugged his waist. "What's the problem?" he asked calmly.

"I want to get married, but Mother won't let us do it for a year. We can't!"

"Why? There's no rush, is there?"

The silence was deafening as Louise and her mother locked eyes. It was broken first by her mother's screeching, followed shortly by fresh sobs from Louise.

"What's happened?" her father shouted over the noise.

"She is going to have a family!" her mother wailed. "Sarah has been hiding her sickness and then she had to tell me!"

His heart stopped as he looked at the two women in his life.

"Let me think," he murmured, swallowing the liquid in his hand.

No, he thought, *not this way. We raised her to be a well-mannered, bright, beautiful woman. A concert pianist, or a member of the established circle of Boston society, seen in the right places with the proper people. Not attached to a hammer-throwing clown. I will deal with him later.*

He turned to JA and said sternly, "You will have to wait for us regardless of your own plans. This has to be done the right way for the sake of our family name."

JA looked down at the floor and said, "I will have to wait then."

Her mother, still shaking but slightly calmer, frowned and said, "Alright. If that is the way it has to be, we must leave right away. I will get Sarah to start packing tonight."

The date was set for November 30th, 1898. Louise had only three bridesmaids because she didn't want the eight her mother had tried to talk her into. JA had Red Angus, and his cousin Blackjack came from the Cape. Because nobody else was available in Boston, he asked Paddy Clark to be in his party.

All the trimmings were there for a wedding. There was a string quartet at the reception, providing the background music. The floral arrangements crowded the walls and set the hallways ablaze with colours. Carriages and servants galore formed a steady progression from the church to the reception. Commotion was the word of the night.

But through all of this, Paddy Clark came to JA's rescue by finding a small staircase where a jar could be enjoyed. JA let Paddy arrange this, as he was busy with the reception line and greeting the influential friends of Louise's mother. The evening came off without a hitch. Later in the evening, Mary and Red Angus teamed up for some Cape songs and dances. At the end of the night, JA and Louise said goodbye to the crowd. As the carriage left, she looked at him and he clutched her to his chest as her tears fell.

Chapter 12

SHE STILL REMEMBERED all the stories he'd told her about the people and the life in the west. Only now she wondered how what she'd heard could be so different from where she found herself. They were living in Stanley with a one-year-old son, and she was pregnant again, sick and always struggling with cleaning and cooking. He left in the morning and did not return to their room until late at night, after he chased the last customer out of the saloon and cleaned up. She was always upset, but then he would take her in his arms and hold her close. She never remembered what he said, but always felt the warmth and security when she fell asleep. JA would look at her, peacefully resting on his chest, and would hope that he was doing her right.

It had been a grind coming here. The train trip had taken two weeks, and then it was a two-and-a-half-day stage trip from Ashcroft. The stage had been crowded, and she'd said that it must have been a year since some of their fellow travellers had bathed. Here the business was slowing down as the rush was over. Most of the men were single and, having no reason to stay, had to move on to survive. Cariboo gold rush, they called it. Stanley was said to be the biggest city in the area, even bigger than Barkerville. They had lived in a tent for two weeks while their room was finished. On one day of those two weeks snow had fallen and it had been bitterly cold.

Vancouver was the new attraction, and everyone seemed to be heading there when the mines or logging camps closed for the winter. He knew Louise was lost without the city and what it offered. Using the hotel to clean clothes and having some women to help her was good, but their husbands were on the move with each season. So he had a choice to make. Jessie was writing from Vancouver and telling him about the prospects. She and Alex were enjoying life there.

This made Louise more upset, and now with Roderick born she was having more angry moments. "This is not what you promised and we planned!" She was demanding more from him. Both were feeling the pressure, and now winter was coming.

Louise had had it one night, and decided to push JA when he came home. She had the kids put to bed, was waiting with a fresh pot of tea and a glass of his favourite scotch. JA could feel the tension when he entered the room. He knew she had been in a mood the past week but tonight was different. She sat at the table without any expression. He took off his coat and wondered what he could say.

"Is something wrong, princess?"

"Something wrong? It is all wrong! I can't take it anymore! You stay away at all day, being front and centre at the hotel, getting all the praise—and I get all the crap! This place is cold, and the kids are busy all the time. You keep saying you'll do something and you do nothing!"

"I provide what I can, and we have enough."

"Well, your enough is nothing. You work your mouth; nobody can smother people with words like you. If we don't move, I will take the boys and move. I should have listened to all those people before we were married."

"You are just tired. Let me plan the move."

"Don't just plan it—do it! And until you do, you are on the couch and the boys are with me in bed."

"No way! This is my house, and I will always have the bed in my house!"

"That is fine for you to say for your manhood," said Louise, walking to the door, "but the boys and I are in the bed and you are not."

Chapter 13

IT WAS NOW 1907, and JA had established himself in the hotel industry. Louise and their three sons—including the youngest, Sandy (or Duncan Alexander Burns, as he was confirmed)—were settled in a house on Helmcken Street near downtown.

JA was now a partner in the Alberta Hotel on Pender Street with another east coaster. His partner had put up most of the money and JA drew clientele to the hotel. This was no problem for JA, as his name was spread around the logging camps and mines as someone who provided a friendly home for all. He now was in charge of the business and his confidence was as big as his stature.

Louise was happy with the boys and the house, but felt left alone as JA spent most of his time at work. The rest of it he spent with the Scottish and Caledonian

Society, a group of Canadian-Scottish men who felt the need to promote their long-ago heritage. But he was always home for Sunday Mass, when they put on their Sunday best and took the boys to the Holy Rosary Church for services. There were always a few relatives of JA—his sister Jessie and her husband Alex, and Crazy Angus from the Cape, plus many more who came and went. JA was always involved with other people and when he was home there were always Capers around to eat their food and drink their liquor. He never let anyone leave without something to quench them. Louise loved to entertain visitors, and would play the piano they had bought at the various impromptu affairs that happened without warning. The boys were enthralled with Crazy Angus and his energy. Another cousin, called Dougald or Blackjack, because he was a gambler in the mines and camps all summer, also joined them often. He was known by the fact that he had a high-water mark: he washed his face and hands, but the dirt still showed on his neck and wrists. Jessie's husband Alex was getting sicker so, other than church on Sunday, they only saw them once a month as they lived up in a new area south of False Creek called Mount Pleasant.

    Louise found her life packed with entertaining all of JA's associates and minding the boys and had little time for herself. But when she was down, he would suddenly be there, smiling and looking at her with those big blue eyes and talking just to her, and she forgot all her woes. She was friends with other mothers and some neighbours, but her Boston background kept them distant as they felt she was above them. The wives of the Scottish and Caledonian group were no friendlier. Some of the group were businessmen whose wives thought they were the socialites of the new Vancouver. Because Louise appreciated the finer side of beer and liquor, and because her outspoken manner had not calmed any, they didn't make Louise feel welcome. So she concentrated on the boys and JA concentrated on the business.

He and his partner were struggling to keep it together. His partner accused JA of giving away their profits with the occasional free beers. The hotel was not being used to its capacity, so the partner decided to sell his share. That left JA without a job. But as it came about, as soon as the word got out, the hotel on Granville Street came to his rescue with a bartending job. JA took the opportunity to continue to draw his clientele and new customers from the south side of the downtown area. He also had more time for the Scottish Society and was involved in raising interest for a new regiment in Vancouver for the Seaforth Highlanders. Some members of the regiments that had fought in the Boer War were taking residence in the area, and his bar was becoming the establishment to hold informal gatherings.

This took more of his time from the house and the boys, but he was getting real satisfaction in doing what made him feel good. When he had any time away from work, he liked to walk up Granville, from Davie to the train station at the north end of downtown. When he walked, he was noticed by many people who stopped him to talk about anything and everything. He liked the attention without the pressure of home or the hotel. He became friends with the liquor distributors, who gave him inside information on what was happening. JA felt that to keep surviving in the fast-paced hospitality business, he had to learn as much as he could and know as many people as he could.

These new friends talked about the business of selling liquor after hours and the money some were making. JA kept all this information in his head, as he thought that it might come to be of use if he was ever out of work. But all this was keeping him from Louise, and their discussions were becoming heated. She still was a determined person, and she told him that she wasn't second fiddle to anyone or anything. Some Sundays were stressful. He was thankful for the boys, as they kept life alive and full of the antics that five-, seven-, and nine-year-olds would get into given any chance. They did answer to their parents, as spankings were a reality, but it was still worth the fun and adventure of living in a big city. JA was not as tolerant as Louise and his short fuse became shorter when he was tired. All this combined to keep him leaning more toward his business dealings and less toward home.

Chapter 14

THE BEER PARLOUR TRADE was a service industry, and JA began to learn about many opportunities outside the hotel doors. His contacts were telling him about the liquor trade that supplied customers with after-hour supplies a little stronger than beer. His connections with the Scottish Society were also involved with the manufacture and distribution of liquor. Things came together more each day.

One day, a supplier offered him the opportunity to buy an excess from other customers—the amount that they would have skimmed from the orders. JA was happy to take him up on the offer. But as he began to arrange storing this liquor at home, Louise was firm. "Definitely not."

He then found that he could use a storeroom at the hotel, as his supplies were not in any great quantity. He also found that a local storage company was willing to give him some space to store stock, as the owner and JA spent time enjoying the fruits of their labours together. Now he just had to figure out how to make their wares available to customers without arousing any suspicion at the hotel—or with the police.

One contact he had was an Italian restaurant owner on Seymour Street who ran a successful distribution of after-hour and weekend supplies from his restaurant's back door. But JA wanted to expand, and to do that he knew he had to find a location unknown to Louise or his employer. The good returns from his meagre supplies were all the incentive he needed to try to expand. He looked at the business area downtown between Main and Granville. He felt he had to be close to both the business and residential areas in the west end of the city. But the location would also need to be free from suspicion by the neighbours and the police. The area east of Main fit these criteria, as it was primarily populated by Japanese and Chinese immigrants who kept very close to each other and kept a low profile from the rest of the city. This would also give him easy access to the area where he would be trading.

He found a house just two blocks from the police station on Gore Avenue. The two-story building had seven rooms besides the bathroom and kitchen. His storage company agreed to provide the means to move the stock as there was never a great amount at any one time. This would also reduce any notice of special activity in the area. With the setup falling into place, he would need someone to stay in the house overnight. He called on his Caper relatives and friends, who spoke Gaelic and owed JA loyalty for his past help. The business was getting set up, and he began quietly communicating among groups looking to buy their after-hours supplies.

Chapter 15

JA WAS WALKING TALL and becoming better known through his work and his association with the Scottish and Caledonian Society. This newfound attention was more than he had known. Others with the Scottish Society gave him more responsibility in gathering support for the proposal of a new regiment. Louise noticed that he was more concerned about his clothes as he became busier with the Society, the hotel, and the Gore Avenue house. He spent less time with her and the boys. "I'm making money," was his standard excuse whenever she brought it to his attention.

As he spent his time talking about everything but the family, she became more demanding. She overheard conversations where he spoke about people she was not familiar with. He talked cheerfully to her about his new friends and their wives, none of whom she had met.

There was a newspaper article with him in the centre of a picture surrounded by two or three women. The women seemed to be gloating over him. When she asked about it, he brushed it off as nothing. But from her point of view, she felt these things were occurring too often. She felt like an outsider in her own home.

Expressing her displeasure in her usual vocal tones left him reeling, and he sought relief by delving further into his business and the Scottish Society. He felt that he was doing what he needed to do, and that fulfilling his goals was going to take determination. The pressure became more extreme from the after-hours business, as the police were always trying to find these operations. The Capers in charge of minding the house in lieu of paying rent were becoming less reliable. Some would go pub crawling, leaving the house empty at night. This was causing problems, as some members of the force were also Scottish Society friends who protected his business for the price of the bottle of prime rye or Scotch that they couldn't afford to buy on their salaries. But when they came after their shift at 2:00 a.m., there would be no one there to provide their bottle. The word got back to JA where he was working at Davie and Granville. He had to send a message to Louise that he wouldn't be home because of having to tend to his business, but Louise knew very little about it and didn't know where he was.

He made the choice to look after his business. So his day became a routine of arriving at home in the morning, resting for a few hours, then cleaning up and going to work at noon at the hotel. It was midnight when he left there. He would go to Gore Avenue and arrange any orders he had to send out. If he had time, he catnapped in the bedroom. A few months into this new schedule, Louise had had enough. The problem had to be resolved.

JA came up with a solution. He told Louise he would let the boys mind the house at night. Louise didn't like the idea, as John was only ten, Rod eight, and Sandy six. JA said that was what was going to happen to keep him in business. He couldn't back out without losing money, and if he did, he couldn't keep providing their needs. She thought back to the horror of living in the Cariboo and realized she had to agree with him for now. So he took John and Rory Beck to the house and told them what he wanted them to do. Sandy was kept at home by Louise as she insisted that he was too young. This alleviated the pressure for the time being.

Now he needed a more permanent program, but that had to wait. Louise was more upset every day as she didn't like the feeling of being neglected. She was becoming more vocal with JA. Her aunt had moved to Seattle, and she was writing to Louise asking her to come visit. The letters gave her a feeling of comfort and security, of home, which seemed to be a long-ago memory.

Chapter 16

THE REGIMENT was coming together. The recruiters had many listed, including the veterans of the Boer War, who were willing to be men of position with the unit. They decided on the Black Watch tartan and received the okay to proceed with all their finery down to the crest and the dirk. The announcement was to come, and a parade of the regiment was arranged for Beatty Street Park with full dress and complement.

They were formed into troops and JA was in group G. Because of his prominent size he was chosen to be in the front row centre for the parade and pictures. That pleased him, and even Louise had to say that he was a fitting sight to see. The kilt he wore was a double size compared to the others.

The Boer members said that if he had been with them, they would have had him in front and they couldn't have been seen. The jokes were easy to make, but they were never said in front of JA, unless there was a quantity of the amber fluids flowing.

Chapter 17

BY 1910, the problems between JA and Louise had grown. JA had become more involved with what he wanted to do and was giving less time to Louise and the boys. JA had been the one making promises, and now those promises were only for JA. Louise had had it with the craziness of the Capers who were showing up and eating and drinking at their expense. Jessie's husband Alex had died, and JA was spending more time with her than with Louise. Jessie was becoming more and more involved in the boys' lives, influencing them in church and school. Louise felt frustrated, left out, and like she wasn't the one responsible for them anymore. Being used to having the run of her life, she decided that the only way to correct the problem was to move to Seattle with her aunt and see if that would wake JA up to the way she was feeling.

When she told him she was going, JA was very upset. He screamed at her about leaving the boys for him to care for.

"I have my business and the regiment and the after-hours customers! I have no time for the raising of an 11-, 9-, and 7-year-old! What do I know about wiping noses and bottoms?!"

"Well," she told him, "now that Jessie is such an important part of your life, she can do it for the time being."

JA turned his back on Louise and told her to go. With an outburst heard all over downtown Vancouver, she let him know what she thought of him as she rode to the train.

"You won't see me until I feel I'm wanted!" were her parting words as she left the city.

"That's good!" JA responded, furious with her. "One less trouble in my life!"

Coldly, he took the boys to Jessie's place on Howe Street. The boys were upset. JA just told them that this was the way it was going to be, and they had to grow up and help each other. They each had to look after the work around the house, and Jessie was strict about attending church and saying prayers each night. This became the pattern of their lives.

JA now was focused on the job and regiment and his other customers. He changed hotels again. He had begun to feel that his bosses thought they owned him, and he responded by becoming more demanding and short with them. He felt he had made his mark in the Scottish and Caledonian Society with the founding of the regiment, and wasn't willing to feel like a servant to them.

His customers were loyal to him, so as he moved around the city, they followed him. His size regularly invited challenges by newcomers to his Beer Parlour, and he had his own way of not getting too involved in any fighting. He would talk his way out of any confrontation by joking or speaking in Gaelic, which always confused drunken customers, or by just using his imposing figure to dissuade them. He would also stand as close to them as he could so they couldn't manoeuvre. He used these deterrents effectively, keeping the bar clear of constant problems.

Chapter 18

THE REGIMENT was at the forefront of JA's mind, as they were progressing toward getting recognition from the other Army units in town. There was a battalion games arranged between the Queen's Own Rifles, the Seaforths, and the Ambulance Battalion for Brockton Oval in Stanley Park. That was to be a great chance for the regiment to show its value. JA was registered in the 56-pound hammer throw, as he'd told them it was what he knew.

He had to get himself ready. He found that he was still in better shape than he would have thought. Lifting kegs, cases of liquor, and all the other labour that goes with working in saloons had kept him trim. As big as he was, he was pretty fit. He was looking forward to the challenge.

He thought about the Cape and the time he had to outthrow Paddy Clark from Boston. He was filled with good memories of Louise, the feeling of being on top of the world, Crazy Angus collecting all the bets. His thoughts moved to how his life was now, back to that day, and over all that had happened since—it made him more determined than ever. Even though he was older, he knew he could do it.

Besides, he could maybe make some money on the side through Crazy Angus. *Oh,* he thought, *I'd better not do that, as the integrity of the troupe is more important, and I may need the Highlanders for future business opportunities.* There was a lot of money in the kilts, as he was finding more at every gathering of the regiment. He was friendly and appealing to be around, so he'd made good, solid connections. He knew a good performance would add to his reputation.

He also knew that he missed Louise, but this would keep his mind off the fact that his marriage was over and he was to be responsible for the boys.

Chapter 19

THE WORLD KEPT CHANGING. The things happening in Europe led to tension against foreign residents. The saloons were still segregated for Asian and Indians and Native Indians. But any non-English-speaking person was being held at arm's length. The regiment was becoming steadfast for king and country with a new king, George V, now installed in England. So the times were for progressing, for building Vancouver, for talking about the future...but everyone was aware of Europe's troubles.

As he prepared himself for the games to come, JA also kept the boys busy running errands. John was a good worker and left school early when he was able to work as a labourer in construction. Rory Beck was not as willing to work, but he helped more with Jessie at home. He also wrote to his mother every week.

Although Sandy was young and still at school, he was eager to please his dad. Always smiling and full of life, he didn't stray from work or from doing anything he was asked to do. They seemed to be settling into life without their mother.

JA still had a busy schedule, but managed to enjoy time with Capers and regiment functions. He was a steady member of the social activities occurring on a weekly basis. He spent no time training the boys, as his life was full. The life they had was going to have to do for now.

The regiment had the parades, and he was happy to be part of the company. They noticed more attention from the public and especially the ladies. The men were beginning to look forward to the gatherings. There was excitement building over the upcoming challenges of the garrison games, and anticipation of showing their colours with the other regiments. The Boer veterans especially wanted to show that they were front and centre, and still an influence in training and building the garrison.

When the day came, the boys came to watch. From the first event—the 100-yard dash—everyone was thrilled with the fact that the participants of the events were so close. This was unusual for events at this time. The bands and colours were so exciting that the boys ran from one place to another to see all the performances. They were awed by the spectacle of the troops together, enthralled at the men in uniform, and felt the pride of their father in his complete outfit. It was even more exciting when he won the hammer throw. Little did they know that his history in that event had shaped their lives.

The games went well, as did the celebration that night. JA enjoyed a big meal and JA a few jars to wash it down.

But as good as the games had been, they wouldn't provide for his family. He found a bartending job at a tourist hotel on Granville, not far from home. Jessie was happy that he was close by in case she needed him for the boys. They were becoming more independent as they pursued their daily work and their own interests. Once a week JA had to provide harsh correction, as they seemed to push the limit—especially when he wasn't there. And they were still spending their nights at the Gore Avenue house. This didn't help their schooling, but they liked the chance to escape school and its regimentation. Sandy in particular enjoyed that he got to meet the different types of characters that revolved around the business. The rich and the hangers-on were interesting to him. The more he was around them, the more he became known as one of JA's kids. Jessie was after him and John all the time to behave themselves. And since they were both no longer altar boys at The Holy Rosary, she prayed every day for their safety. JA's businesses kept them busy following him around.

But JA was finally settled into a steady job with a good boss. He still paraded himself when he could, and there were many opportunities with all the celebrations in the city. When they were presenting the colours of the regiment, the Scottish and Caledonian Society took part in the parade, and JA rode on their float through the downtown and over the new Georgia Viaduct. He was given so many photographs and cards after this that he realized his position in the community had been boosted. Louise may not have been around, but his life was filled...though he was continually reminded by Jessie and the boys of her part in their lives. If he had time to dwell on it, he would allow himself to smile when he thought about how many times she'd scolded him and they'd ended up in an embrace.

Chapter 20

ON THE DAY in April 1913 when the Titanic sank, everyone was in shock. The bar was full of people exchanging theories and stories about the boat and the passengers. News was coming in over the telegraph wires, and newspapers were selling out as quickly as they appeared on the street. That night, the boys in the back of the saloon called to JA that his son was there. He couldn't imagine why one of the boys would come to the bar. He went out back and there was Sandy, smiling from ear to ear and black all over his face and hands.

"Dad. I sold four copies of the paper today! I sold them all! What should I do with the money?" JA couldn't help but smile at the scruffy-looking 10-year-old, who was so excited he couldn't stand in one spot. He thought for a moment and replied, "Give it to Jessie to hold for you. But take a penny for each of you boys and buy a treat." JA would always remember how proud Sandy was that day. He thought it was too bad that Louise wasn't there to share the moment.

As the new year approached, Europe was in turmoil. Each week brought more news about the problems between the governments. And each week the national pride became more evident. The regiment was formed, and all were discussing what they would do if a war came. In the saloon, there were differing opinions, with some saying it wasn't going to happen and some saying it was inevitable. At church and in the saloon, all were asking him what he would be doing. He never answered directly.

JA kept himself busy with the bar and the Gore Avenue dispensary. These were giving him some financial stability. He was saving money and looked to see if there was an opportunity for him to start a business. A possible opportunity came up in Victoria and he took a few days to see how it was.

When he got back Jessie asked, "How was Victoria?"

"Too many kippers for me," was his answer.

But he did come back with a walking stick. It had an ivory globe on the top with a five-inch circumference, and a knotted wood shaft, five feet long, that was polished and shiny. He would only take it to church. The boys loved it, but they couldn't use it themselves as it towered above them. They were full of questions about his trip and the stick.

"I bought it at a tobacconist store called EA Morris. There was an amazing thing in the store, a real wonderful cigar-lighting machine. This was in the middle of the store, and it was fired by gas. You bit the end off the cigar and lit it on the flame. There is only one other like it, at a hotel in Singapore." The boys were amazed, and thought about faraway places. But they had enough stories of wonder closer to home from the Capers who told tales of mining and logging camps. There were stories of card games, of hard work in damp, cold spaces. The big trees and huge Douglas fir logs would stay in their minds and hearts forever.

Chapter 21

THE GREAT WAR ARRIVED, and the turmoil in the city was startling. This had been a year of tension and strife, including the *Komagata Maru* incident, where a ship of East Indian immigrants was denied entry and forced to return to Calcutta, as well as a strike of many factions of unemployed residents.

JA had been busy with parades of the regiment at the Beatty Street grounds, and showings of the Battalion in Stanley Park. The call to arms was now at a fever pitch, with work and the dispensary keeping him wishing he was a twin. His boss was also demanding more time to keep the hotel up to the level he expected. With all these pulls on his time, JA's boys got lost in the shuffle. He knew they were still going to church, but they also were starting to spread their wings to get work for wages. John had become a labourer, Rory Beck was delivering for a store, and Sandy just kept himself busy doing anything that he could to make a nickel.

Hastings Street, a few short blocks from the Gore Avenue house, had become the focal point of business in the city. Stores were opening, selling many varieties of goods, and people were always on the street. New areas sprouted across False Creek, opening up the Jitney traffic along with the street cars. While around him businesses were booming, JA was feeling the crush of the lack of supplies available for his dispensary. The area was becoming a much more high-traffic spot, popular for liquor and ladies of the night, so it was not as attractive as when he'd started there. And all these new city boundaries and traffic had caused the pressure to grow. Time was against him, so he sold the location to another, bigger retailer with more staff and customers.

One day Jessie stopped him, insisting he take a minute to listen to her. "You need some changes in your life. You are just working and parading, and you are missing life. Louise has settled in Seattle and John goes to see her with Rory Beck. She knows them more than you do!"

"I know that, but I have to provide for us, and it is necessary to work. I will keep working. The boys know where I am, and they need to learn to look after themselves. I will teach them all I know about work—life will teach them the rest every day."

Jessie scowled but didn't argue. "I will keep them in church and make sure they say their prayers. Sandy will be the most trouble, as he is always looking for any excuse to avoid school."

"Don't worry about him. He will learn to fend for himself, and I will teach him the trade if it comes to that."

For all his insistence, JA realized that Jessie was right. He was spending all his time making a living and a name for himself—would his friends still be there when he had time? But he didn't dwell on it. He had to keep on surviving, so he concentrated on work.

FIRST PUBLIC APPEARANCE OF 72ND HIGHLANDERS, CORONATION DAY, 22ND JUNE, 1911

Chapter 22

NOVEMBER 11TH, 1918, arrived with the headline "The War is Over!"

The bar became the most boisterous that JA had ever seen, with crying, laughing, emotionally drained people coming together for days at a time. People hugged and kissed strangers they had just met. Bagpipe and violin music filled the streets. Business was thriving with overflowing crowds, and JA worked until late at night—sometimes sleeping on the floor, with a quick wash in a basin with a cloth being the most luxurious clean up available.

The regiment decided to have a show of colours. JA had to decide between work and wearing the kilt as part of the parade. As he was trying to make up his mind, he was pressured by the owner for more work. He responded, "I quit."

He returned to Jessie's house, bathed, and had a good night's rest. The next morning, he prepared himself for the parade, polishing buckles and brooches, shining the dirk and his boots. He was meticulous in the details. The last task—and the most important—was to trim and clip the moustache and eyebrows and make sure all was correct.

The parade marshalled at the Beatty Street grounds across from the Armoury. The band was full of glory and spirit and the troops were straight, prime, and polished. JA was front and centre. He enjoyed the attention that the uniform gave him. He felt alive.

JA wasn't worried about finding work. Prohibition in Canada had been in force for two years, with little or no effect on the liquor business—other than promoting the operation of unlicensed houses. So JA had many opportunities to find work. He enjoyed himself as the festivities carried on until Jessie got upset, reminding him of who he was and what he had to do.

About three weeks went by. One day after Mass at the Cathedral, JA, John, and Jessie went to lunch (Rory Beck and Sandy were working out of town). At the restaurant, JA informed them of his plans to go into business for himself. "There's a shop on Powell Street that is available. It sold liquor and cigarettes, plus it has a small area for eating sandwiches and drinks." John was excited at his dad's choice. "It sounds great! Maybe I could get out of this labouring and logging stuff, which is tough and always dirty."

"I wanted to talk you into joining me and I am glad to hear you like the idea," JA said with a smile. When Jessie excused herself to go to the ladies' room, JA added, "There's something I should tell you, John. The last owners were shut down due to illegal sales. That is why it is so cheap. But by using the buffet as a front, we can operate quietly and should be able to make some backdoor money."

"I should have known we would be offering more than food with you, Dad."

"Just don't tell Jessie. She doesn't need any more reasons to offer prayers and light candles."

"How long before we start?"

"Pretty quick. We just have to count the stock and sign the papers. I might need your help, because they might just count it and take it out the back door."

"Good idea. How about we go tomorrow and get it done quickly?"

Jessie returned and they told her of their ideas to start as soon as possible. She was delighted. Beaming proudly on them, she said, "My prayers for you two are being answered."

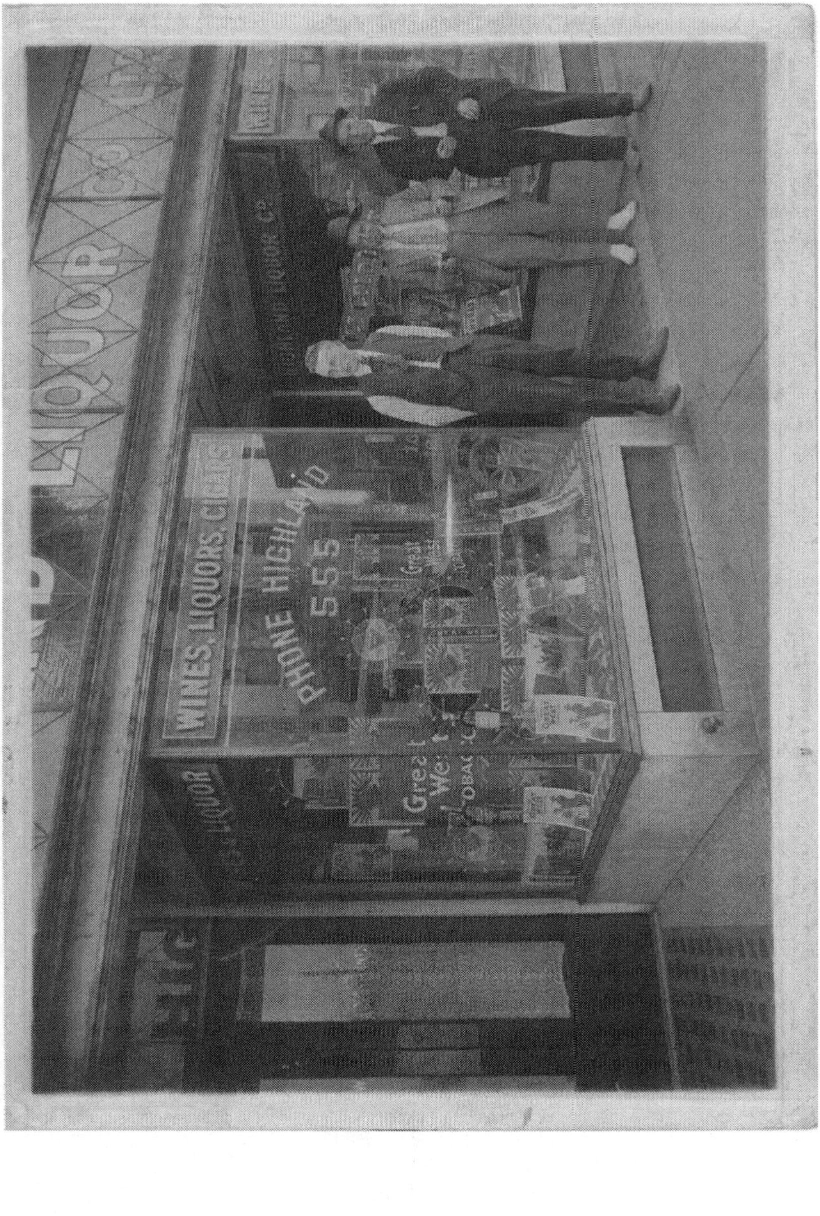
WINES, LIQUORS, CIGARS
PHONE HIGHLAND
555
LIQUOR

Chapter 23

HIGHLAND LIQUOR STORE, *Purveyor of Fine Wines, Beer, and Spirits,* said the advertisement.

It was operating fine as a buffet, with JA handling the supplies and the pricing, while John did the day-to-day selling. That left JA time to look into other business opportunities around the city. He became acquainted with those in the regiment who had money from dealing in the illegal trade. At Mass every Sunday, he was surprised to find both the regiment and trade members becoming more affiliated in the church meetings. The more people he became associated with and the more he widened his knowledge, the more sure he became that he could survive without going behind the bar anymore. He looked to work the front end and manage, but not labour. He thought things were starting to look better; but he knew he had felt that way before with Louise and it didn't last. He wouldn't let it get away again.

When he was meeting people at church and other social events, he began to notice the same woman was always there. She started to register more and more with him, until one day he asked the priest about her.

"Her name is Mary," he said. "Lovely woman. A widow. Her husband died in an accident. Very sad."

After that, JA seemed to see her once a week somewhere: the Hudson Bay Company, Woodward's, stores on Hastings Street. She was quiet, polite, and very graceful. To his mind, she was the opposite to Louise—but then again, Stanley may have taken the shine off Louise. Mary was medium height, always neat and orderly, and there was something about her that attracted him. He felt he would like to just talk to her. *A simple hello would probably be okay...but don't stand so close to her that you scare her, and make sure you watch your language.* Then it dawned on him: he would get Jessie to introduce him at church after Mass. That would be the perfect setting.

And she did just that. "Mary, this is my brother, James Angus. I thought I should introduce you."
Mary said, "Pleased to meet you officially. I have seen you here and at the troop socials. They have you in the forefront at all the parades. I felt I knew you."

"I am pleased to meet you, Mary. I have seen you around too."

The conversation moved along, congenial and relaxed, when all of a sudden Crazy Angus appeared out of nowhere, blurting, "Where do we meet today, JA?"

"Probably at Jessie's on Howe Street," JA hurriedly replied.

"See you there, and I will get more to come!" he shouted, disappearing as suddenly as he had come. JA stood still, wondering if his chance had just been ruined.

"Quite a ball of energy," Mary said gently.

Right then JA knew all was good.

Chapter 24

JA MARRIED MARY and they settled in the new area of Commercial Drive near the interurban train. He was able to take the train to work in a short time, and the Central Station was right at the centre of the Hastings Street commercial centre.

Activities in the east part of Main Street were growing in the illegal trade, and it was attracting many kinds of illicit trade and traffic. Business at the Highland was not as good as expected, and JA was approached by the previous owner, asking if he was willing to sell it back. JA would still manage it for him, but the owner would be responsible for the money end of the business. John decided that he wanted to go to Seattle, where Louise had also remarried. He felt there were more prospects for work there, and besides, he felt he needed to be on his own. So once again, JA was on the lookout for future prospects for work. But now in his fifties, he wasn't as fit as he had been in previous years.

At Mass one Sunday, he was approached by an Italian member to ask if he would be interested in working as a partner with him. The provincial government was introducing new rules and regulations for the hotels and how they were allowed to provide liquor to customers. Now, there was to be sales of beer only, separate rooms for men and for ladies, and no music or entertainment allowed. It was to be a complete change to the drinking habits and open practices the hotel industry had previously enjoyed. Prohibition was ending, but leftover pressure from the female population was showing in the legislation coming down. Applications were being submitted, and the Italian partner was looking for well-known citizens submit their names on the applications. JA was a prime candidate, because not only was he well-known, he also had friends in the regiment who had some influence with the legislature. He was a perfect front man on any license request. JA felt that it was an opportunity for him to survive without labour-intensive work. He also enjoyed the thought of being a partner. Mary would be pleased with his position and the fact he would always be well-dressed for his work. With John gone and Sandy roaming the woods doing odd jobs, they had a quiet, relaxed time to enjoy their new life.

Sandy came back to town that winter and stayed downtown. He had spent a few months with Louise in Seattle on his way home. Because of his work, he had developed an attitude—and he could back it up. He had built his strength working and learned how to box. He had defended himself in the camps quite well, and his confidence had grown. The story that Rory Beck told JA was that John and Sandy had been imbibing in Seattle when they heard about the Golden Gloves boxing tournament being held. John pestered Sandy until, before he knew it, he was fighting the next Friday night. Rory Beck mentioned that it was a funny sight to see: Sandy was in the ring and his face dropped when he turned around and saw his opponent. The fellow was 50 pounds heavier and looked to be forty years old, with a large scar on his cheek. Sandy didn't say anything, but when the bell sounded, he advanced sternly. The big man swung and Sandy went down. The count came to 10 and the bell sounded again. Sandy got up and went to the corner, where John asked if he was hurt. "Hell no. Just the wind from the swing going by my chin was enough to tell me to get out of here. Let's leave, I need a drink."

JA ribbed Sandy all the time about being KOed by the wind of a blow. He always smiled when the story was told in the hotels.

JA heard that Louise and her husband had had a baby girl born to them. He thought it odd that they'd called her Jessie, but then he heard that her husband had a relative by that name and Louise had an Aunt Jessie as well, so it was a good choice. He felt that Louise now had her life, and he could allow himself not to feel worry or guilt anymore. When he arrived home, Mary was always ready with tea and milk. There was peace to his life. Even when he was sometimes delayed by work, there was still tea and the calm welcome that made him relax. Again, life seemed to be good

In 1923, the licenses were issued. Much to his amazement, there was James Angus named on two Hotel Beer Parlour licenses out of the first 10 issued for the city of Vancouver. The regiment noticed his position in the hotel industry and some members began talking to him about their old connections in the liquor trade. Other members were also in the business of distilling and brewing beer and spirits. With prohibition going strong in the USA, the prospect of increasing sales south of the border was becoming real.

JA knew that his hotel connections may be over after the hotels were up and running. So he began finding out what was needed to import liquor into the USA. The first thing he realized was that he would need connections on the coast of Washington and Oregon. He remembered that there was a regiment show of colours in the Tacoma Armory coming up in the next six months. He hadn't planned to go, but now he thought it was a must. He should be able to muster some support from the other regiments there and make connections. That is what happened: he found many from the area north of Seattle up to Bellingham and also down the Washington coast East of Olympia. The area had lots of small bays and drop-off points away from the areas of police control, and many fishermen who would be able to land their "catch" without being scrutinized. Through these new friends he also discovered many uncharted bays and inlets that would allow much to be done.

On the home side, he needed to make sure there were vessels available for transport. They had many well-built yachts, the pleasure crafts of yacht club members, available to them. But in order to outmanoeuvre the American agents, they needed upgrading.

JA met with a family of industrial electrical installers. They engineered a way to rewire the motors to increase engine capacity. The boats were delivered at night to private homes in good residential areas. Large driveways and garages kept the improvements quiet.

All was ready to go.

He kept all this from Mary, as the less she knew, the less danger there was for her. As far as his wife knew, he was just running the hotels and managing the buffet when needed. Going on his out-of-town trips became a monthly sojourn to make arrangements and pay the handlers. The Capers who had immigrated to the Washington coast area to fish spoke to him in Gaelic; if anyone overheard their conversation, it was just two foreigners chatting. The only precaution they took was not allowing it to be a matter of public knowledge. Some Capers were extra talkative, so they were kept out of the plans. The US agents were always on the alert for any rumours floating around that might help them catch the importers.

Chapter 25

IT WAS THE ROARING TWENTIES and people were spending more than they were earning. They were unrestrained for the first time anyone could remember. Prohibition was in full swing in the US, and JA was ready for the prospects he had been planning to come to fruition.

The boats were ready and the crews set. They started the runs. One of the captains, known as "Captain Matty," was a big Scotsman (but not a Caper). He and JA had known each other for ten years, as he was a regular in JA's establishments. They had become close friends and trusted each other.

JA's connections on the Washington and Oregon coast made his trips more perilous, as the local county law officers varied in their enforcement. One sheriff near Bellingham was very diligent about seeking out smugglers doing business in his area. JA used the excuse that he was travelling to Seattle to see his son as the reason for his many excursions. He did not want to stop traveling, as it would have curtailed his income, but he knew he was taking chances.

The close call came when he was traveling on the Chuckanut Drive with Sandy. The drive was restricted by a forest fire. Knowing that the sheriff was in the area and questioning everyone about what they were doing there, he told Sandy, "Drive on and don't stop unless we have to because of the road!" As they drove, Sandy had to swerve around, avoiding downed trees and burning bushes.

"The floorboards are burning!" Sandy yelled.

"Keep going! Keep on the road!" JA cried out as he stamped the boards with his boots.

Sandy drove the hairpins like he had engineered them, driving around fire scraps and trees until he finally exited the Chuckanut. He kept his foot to the floor as they headed north toward the Bellingham. "Don't go too fast or attract any attention," was all JA said.

As he drove through Bellingham, he was glad to see the city in the rearview mirror. Efforts like this increased JA's reputation as someone reliable and trustworthy with the others in the group.

JA was enjoying the fact he and Mary were able to live quietly in Burnaby, away from the business of downtown. She showed her English upbringing in the way she hosted any friends that ventured out to visit them: always ready with cakes and tea served in proper cup-and-saucer sets. JA found it very relaxing. He also liked having the yard to look after, and that they had all the necessary things for their comfort. But he was worried about where his next income would come from when these business partnerships were over.

He had Sandy working as a waiter in the hotel on Cordova. Sandy was very gregarious, which made him a natural for dealing with the public. He liked to meet people and was always looking for ways to increase his income and keep employed. John had settled in Seattle and Rory Beck was still in Arizona, chasing his dream of being in the movies, doing westerns. So JA just had to worry about providing for himself and Mary.

Chapter 26

JA WAS NOT SURPRISED when Sandy got a job with Checker Cabs. Being a waiter was not easy when you had to deal with the drinkers. Sandy wasn't aggressive, and although he handled himself well, he wasn't happy when he had to act as peacemaker or bouncer.

Sandy said to JA, "I really enjoy meeting the people from the trains and boats. The trips to the hotels and restaurants when they are spruced up in their finery is always a good feeling." JA was not even thinking about it, but Sandy was talking about the restaurant at Hastings in Granville quite a bit. This was a meeting place with a big eating area. Visitors started their trips here. Sandy mentioned the Aussies and Kiwis, how they loved beer and good times well into the mornings. He seemed to be enjoying himself, but then again, he always did wherever he was and whoever he was with. JA mentioned the change in Sandy and Mary said, "It sounds like he has met a girl."

When he saw Sandy next and mentioned it, Sandy just smiled and said, yes, he was interested in a waitress called Edna. JA had a shock coming when he found out Edna was German and Lutheran! Sandy was stubborn and had always had his own mind, so JA knew there was no use in discussing it with him. But he bemoaned to himself that there were so many Catholic girls at the Rosary and the new Catholic Church at Main and 12th, and this was who he had to choose. It was almost as bad as going with an Irish or English girl.

The point seemed to disappear when Sandy came to him and said, "We are going to be married at St. Patrick's Church just after Christmas, but I need to borrow some money for the license and the priest."

The wedding went off well. Edna's sister and family supplied the food, and JA the liquor. Sandy was happy when Rory Beck stood up with him and John came from Seattle. Louise didn't make it; she said it was too long a trip to take with her baby.

Chapter 27

1928 ENDED with Sandy and Edna having a daughter named after Louise. Everybody was doing well, and Sandy was newly employed as a streetcar conductor, which meant regular work and pay.

Mary and JA were enjoying the farm-like atmosphere in Burnaby, with only the Interurban to break the solitude. Mary had regular Sunday dinners of potatoes, peas and carrots, and roast beef with the meat well done for JA. After dinner, he and whoever was visiting—Capers or people who needed a temporary home—would retire to the living room for a cigar and a glass of Scotch. Conversation may have been broken by a radio show; JA liked comedies and detective stories. Most nights they listened to Mary's classical recordings, which soothed the atmosphere for JA. But whenever he was enjoying himself or had a few extra drinks, he would play his Harry Lauder recording, do the Cape Breton dancing, and laugh and smile. When he joined in, singing with his big voice, it sent flocks of birds skywards. He knew every word of every song and lived every nuance and phrase. After these nights Mary always smiled as she watched him, laid out on his back, completely relaxed, and snoring loudly with a huge smile on his face.

1929 progressed, and there was no slowing to people making and spending money. Rory Beck was back at work locally, changing jobs in an effort to find one that he liked. JA worried about him.

One rainy September night, Rory Beck came to JA at the buffet.

"Crazy Angus has gone a tear, and none of his friends have seen him for a few days. The Capers are organizing a search to try and trace his last known whereabouts." He sighed, and went on, "The police laughed when the Capers reported him missing because they said he was always missing. But they did say they would tell patrols to keep a watch for him."

JA got hold of the regiment to help in looking out for Angus, with no luck. Two days later, Rory Beck came back with the news that someone had seen him at the Victory Square Cenotaph. He was naked, saying his rosary. Someone called the ambulance and as far as they knew he'd been taken away for government care.

Then came the crash. It was October 1929, and it sent everyone scrambling to recover any of the money they had been spending. The crowds still came to the beer parlour, but the atmosphere was much more serious. The rounds were slower to finish and when they were done people just sat and continued with their conversations. Tips were scarce, if any.

As the new year progressed, people with jobs did whatever was necessary to keep them. Those without jobs walked the streets, knocking on doors, looking for anyone who knew about any possibility of work. JA was giving credit to people he knew, and started to provide overnight rooms for those without lodging to share. To help them keep their dignity, he had the barber in the hotel give them shaves and haircuts at half price (thus the phrase "shave and a haircut, two bits").

    John was still in Seattle, married now, and working the docks steady. Louise and her husband were doing well with their fishing boat. JA was glad he and Mary had the rented property, but they knew that the owner planned to sell. They didn't know how much time they had left.

Chapter 28

1929 AND 1930 were years that would be remembered as the most desperate and shocking of all their lives. Things were never the same. Survival became the topic of each day. The buffet at the hotel became a soup kitchen, and the rooms were used to house the homeless. The partners were getting very little revenue, but they took what they could as there was no alternative. JA was working hard to find the balance between his income and his conscience. The hotel was barely making it, but so many people were struggling, living right on the edge of despair.

He was forced to make hard choices for himself and Mary. The Burnaby property sold, and they moved to a house in the Dunbar area on the west side of Vancouver, where a regiment member was looking for a reliable tenant to maintain the property and cover the expenses. JA was still making trips to the US for his contacts, using his Caper connections to keep the traffic moving as much as they could while the pressure increased. This income helped JA and Mary not only keep themselves, but help others survive. *"Keep right on to the end of the road,"* Harry Lauder sang on the record. It was the struggle everyone faced, but at least JA felt better after a cup of amber liquid and an hour listening to Harry Lauder.

The hotel business was getting squeezed tighter, and there were no new opportunities. JA decided he couldn't be as lenient with drinks or rooms as he had been. The owners were cutting more expenses; his workday became longer and there was more physical work than he had been doing. He was getting to the point of needing more rest. Mary suggested that he slow down and use his experience to make a change to something less stressful. He made the switch to running the hotel, leaving the beer parlour to the younger ones. But he was always called in when his expertise was needed. Hiring staff, managing people, and keeping the premises up to standard were the things he couldn't let go. Proper rules of management were a part of him.

Even when he finally quit the business altogether, he still went to town two or three days a week to check on what was happening.

Chapter 29

THE SECOND WORLD WAR started, and again, JA helped the regiment get ready. People had begun to work, and the hotels were profitable enough to hire more staff. He couldn't sit still, and he told Mary, "I shall continue to help the cause as much as I can." Still wearing his hat and carrying his walking stick, he was a formidable sight as he walked the business districts of Granville and Hastings. This was emphasized even more when he strode through Chinatown, and the small children ran away from the "big white giant."

His funds were running low, so he and Mary moved to a smaller house in Burnaby. Here he had to cut wood for the furnace and stove and work in the yard. Mary continued to be ready to entertain the king and queen if they happened to come by. JA was content because the humble little house was always inviting and comfortable.

One rainy June day he came home to see the log pile dwindling. Taking off his suit, he went out to chop firewood without a shirt. About two weeks later, he was not breathing right, and Mary called him a doctor.

"You have pneumonia, JA," said the doctor, shaking his head. "You are not as young as you think you are, and you have to be careful. There's not much I can do except tell you to rest and drink plenty of liquids—and not your favourite kind, either. Just water or tea. Sit as much as you can, and don't lay down unless you are sleeping."

JA knew the doctor was right. He did feel his age. But he was determined to keep going. He made the Interurban trip to the city three times a week and went to church most Sundays. It took a full day to travel, have the service, and visit, so sometimes he wasn't up to it. Mary became worried as winter approached, as JA was struggling to keep the wood supply up. Rory Beck and Sandy would come out to help, but they were both working long hours and not available enough.

After JA had another spell, Sandy approached the two of them. He told JA, "I have enough room at my house to have you come there to recover. Edna will help even if she does have five children." He told JA that there was no question about it. They would have their room, their own space, and could have any visitors they liked. JA was upset; he didn't want to admit that he couldn't look after himself.

"Look, Dad," Sandy said, "it is only short-term. And when you get your strength back, you can do whatever you want."

The arrangement worked well. JA and Mary kept away from Edna, and Edna kept the kids away from JA. But every morning Edna brought JA a boiled egg, unbroken, in a cup, along with a clean glass for his drink of whiskey. "I don't want her touching my food," he told Mary. She said "Okay, I will make sure I taste it first." Mary thought this was slightly bizarre but figured that JA could not trust Germans after the war experience. The days went on.

Until one morning, they didn't. Mary called frantically for Rory Beck, "Come! Come quickly!" When he got to their room, he saw JA, laying on his back, his legs extended beyond the end of the bed—not breathing. He was cold. They called the doctor, who confirmed that JA had passed away.

Sandy came home from work, crying as he entered the house. They made the funeral arrangements through their tears. The mourners came to the house for the next few days, filling the two floors as they exchanged stories while Edna fed them and Sandy filled their glasses.

JA was laid to rest in a plot overlooking the city he had provided with a touch of Caper hospitality, Caper worth ethic, and Caper history.

Epilogue

LOUISE HEARD ABOUT JA passing and phoned Sandy to say she wouldn't be able to make the trip as everyone was busy. She also mentioned that she would be looking for a portion of the estate and she planned to hire a lawyer.

Sandy replied, "Don't waste your money. After we paid for the doctor and the funeral, there was nothing left. That is why he was here."

Louise was last seen in Vancouver at Sandy's funeral, wearing a purple Husky pom after spending the weekend with one of her beaus on the 50-yard line at Husky Stadium.

Mary moved in with her son in Dunbar.

Edna put all the regiment trappings in a trunk at the foot of the basement stairs. From the dirk to the badges and kilt, they filled the whole trunk. Eventually, the Vancouver Police Band came and bought the trunk and all the supplies it held. Sandy heard JA's kilt became the kilts for two members of the band.

In Judique, Inverness County, Nova Scotia, the news was given to Annie MacDermid. Red Angus had had a stroke two years previously, and sat in his rocking chair overlooking the bay. Annie read a newspaper to him once a week but had not had a response since his stroke. She stood before him and said, "Red, JA has passed away."

A small tear appeared on his cheek, and then he smiled and said:

> "He's a broad, broad hi'land laddie name of JA.
> There is no one else like him till this very day.
> You could always tell he was a Scottish built
> by the wig wig waggle of his kilt."